W9-BXN-309

SUPER SIMPLE BODY

INSIDE
THE
KIDNEYS

KARIN HALVORSON, M.D.

Consulting Editor, Diane Craig, M.A./Reading Specialist

Super Sandcastle

An Imprint of Abdo Publishing
abdopublishing.com

Peachtree

VISIT US AT ABDOPUBLISHING.COM

Published by Abdo Publishing, a division of ABDO, PO Box 398166, Minneapolis, Minnesota 55439. Copyright © 2016 by Abdo Consulting Group, Inc. International copyrights reserved in all countries. No part of this book may be reproduced in any form without written permission from the publisher. Super SandCastle™ is a trademark and logo of Abdo Publishing.

Printed in the United States of America,
North Mankato, Minnesota
102015
012016

THIS BOOK CONTAINS
RECYCLED MATERIALS

Editor: Liz Salzmann
Content Developer: Nancy Tuminelly
Cover and Interior Design: Mighty Media, Inc.
Photo Credits: Shutterstock

Library of Congress Cataloging-in-Publication Data
Halvorson, Karin, 1979- author.
 Inside the kidneys / Karin Halvorson, M.D. ; consulting editor, Diane Craig, M.A./reading specialist.
    pages cm. -- (Super simple body)
 ISBN 978-1-62403-943-0
1. Kidneys--Juvenile literature. 2. Urine--Juvenile literature. I. Title.
II. Series: Halvorson, Karin, 1979- Super simple body.
 QP249.H35 2016
 612.4'63--dc23
                        2015020589

Super SandCastle™ books are created by a team of professional educators, reading specialists, and content developers around five essential components—phonemic awareness, phonics, vocabulary, text comprehension, and fluency—to assist young readers as they develop reading skills and strategies and increase their general knowledge. All books are written, reviewed, and leveled for guided reading and early reading intervention programs for use in shared, guided, and independent reading and writing activities to support a balanced approach to literacy instruction.

NOTE TO ADULTS

THIS BOOK is all about encouraging children to learn the science of how their bodies work! Be there to help make science fun and interesting for young readers. Many activities are included in this book to help children further explore what they've learned. Some require adult assistance and/or permission. Make sure children have appropriate places where they can do the activities safely.

Children may also have questions about what they've learned. Offer help and guidance when they have questions. Most of all, encourage them to keep exploring and learning new things!

CONTENTS

YOUR BODY

YOUR KIDNEYS

You're amazing! So is your body!
Your body has a lot of different parts. Your kidneys, skin, blood, muscles, and bones all work together every day. They keep you moving. Even when you don't realize it.

The human body has two kidneys (KID-neez). They keep your body healthy and clean! They work 24 hours a day, 7 days a week.

Some people only have one kidney. That's okay! You only need one kidney to live!

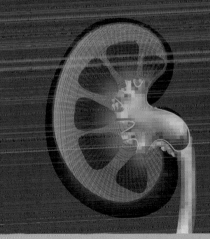

THE INSIDE OF A KIDNEY

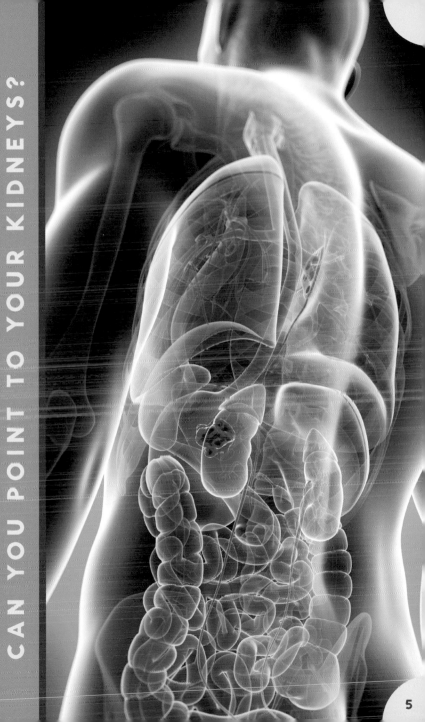

ALL ABOUT THE
KIDNEYS

A kidney looks like a giant kidney bean. That's how the bean got its name.

KIDNEY BEANS

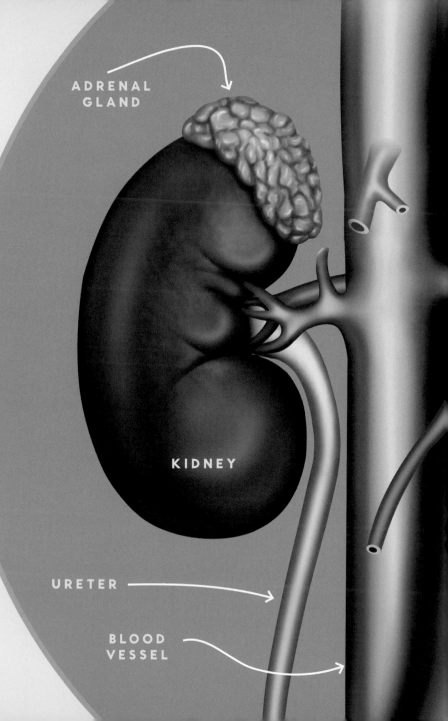

ADRENAL GLAND

KIDNEY

URETER

BLOOD VESSEL

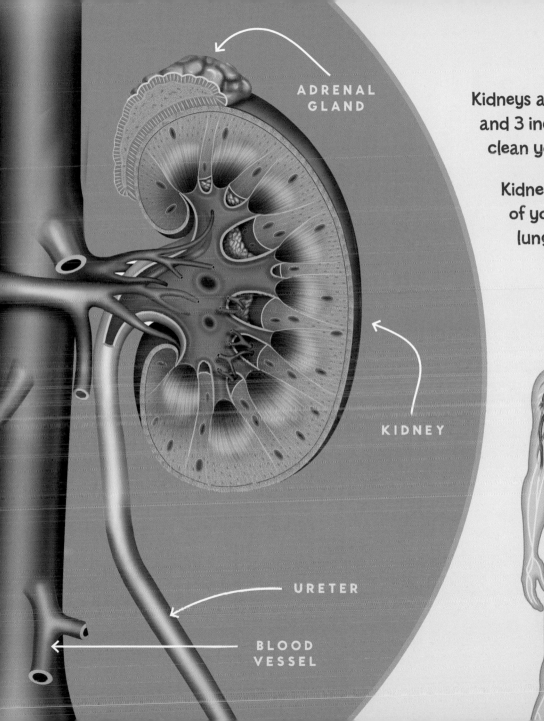

ADRENAL
GLAND

KIDNEY

URETER

BLOOD
VESSEL

Kidneys are 5 inches (12.5 cm) long and 3 inches (7.5 cm) wide. They clean your blood.

Kidneys are near the lowest part of your back. Your heart and lungs sit above your kidneys.

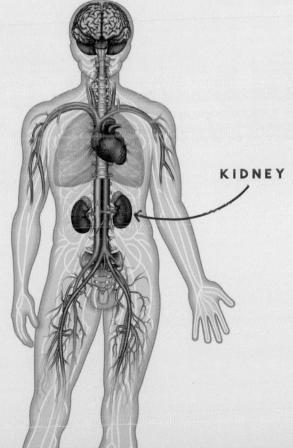

KIDNEY

SO FRESH, SO CLEAN

Your heart pumps blood through your **blood vessels.** The blood vessels take the blood throughout your body. They take blood to your kidneys.

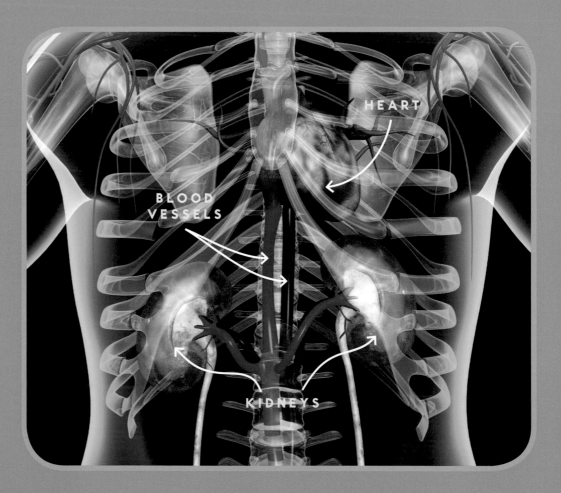

HEART

BLOOD VESSELS

KIDNEYS

The **blood vessels** in your kidneys branch out. They get smaller and smaller. The branches have **filters.**

The filters clean your blood. They take things you don't need out of the blood. They send the clean blood back through your body.

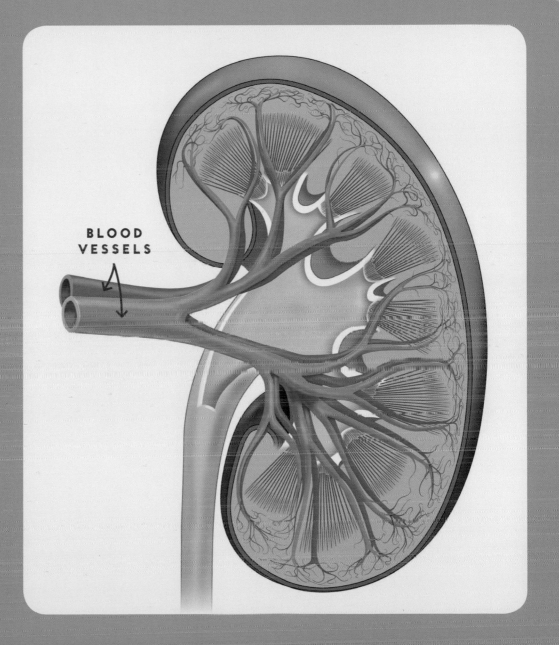

BLOOD VESSELS

TEENY TINY
FILTERS

The **filters** in your kidneys are called nephrons (NEF-ronz). They are tiny. You can only see them with a microscope. But you have a lot of them! Each of your kidneys has one million nephrons!

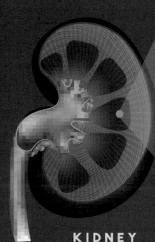

KIDNEY

FAST FACT

You have about 1½ **gallons** (5.5 L) of blood in your body. Your kidneys filter that blood 300 times a day!

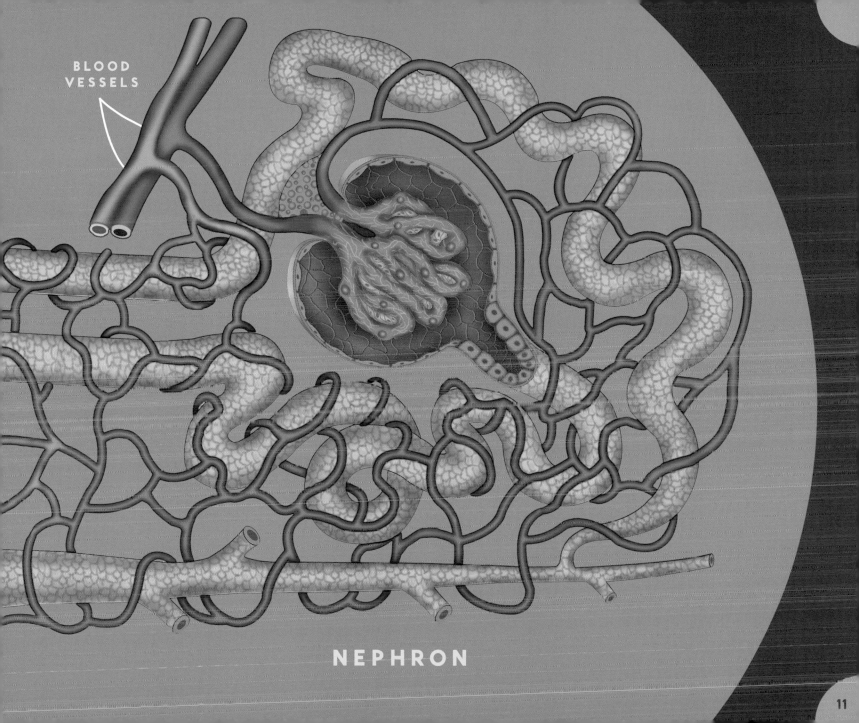

BLOOD
VESSELS

NEPHRON

FILTERING FUN

THE FILTER IN YOUR BODY

WHAT YOU NEED: 2-LITER PLASTIC BOTTLE, SCISSORS, 2-CUP MEASURING CUP, 2 CUPS COTTON BALLS, 1 CUP SAND, 1 CUP GRAVEL, SHEET OF PAPER, FOOD COLORING

HOW TO DO IT

1. Remove the cap from the bottle. Cut the bottle in half. Put the top half of the bottle upside down in the bottom half.

2. Put the cotton balls in the top half. Pour the sand over the cotton balls. Pour the gravel on top of the sand.

3. Put 1 cup of water in the measuring cup. Tear the paper into small pieces. Add the paper to the water. Add a few drops of food coloring.

4. Pour the water over the gravel.

WHAT'S HAPPENING?

Look at the water in the bottom of the bottle. It is less colorful and doesn't have paper in it. The cotton, sand, and gravel work like the nephrons in kidneys. They clean the water.

SALTS

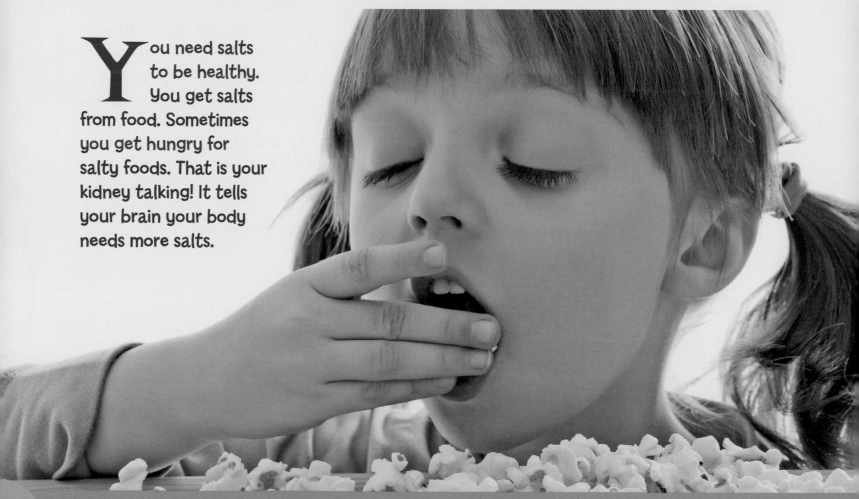

You need salts to be healthy. You get salts from food. Sometimes you get hungry for salty foods. That is your kidney talking! It tells your brain your body needs more salts.

Scientists call the salts in our body electrolytes (i-lek-TRUH-litez). Electrolytes are important. They help every single cell in your body work!

Acids and **bases** are electrolytes when they are in a liquid, such as blood. Electrolytes are called electrolytes because they conduct electricity. The energy they give off is either positive or negative. If it is positive, the electrolyte is an acid. If the energy is negative, the electrolyte is a base.

Acid electrolytes

POTASSIUM (*PUH-tas-ee-uhm*)

SODIUM (*SOH-dee-uhm*)

CALCIUM (*KAL-see-uhm*)

MAGNESIUM (*mag-NEE-zee-uhm*)

Base electrolytes

BICARBONATE (*bye-KAHR-buh-nate*)

CHLORIDE (*KLOR-ide*)

PHOSPHATE (*fahs-FATE*)

SULFATE (*suhl-FATE*)

BICARBONATE BOMB

MAKE ELECTROLYTES BOOM!

WHAT YOU NEED: PAPER NAPKIN, MEASURING SPOONS, 1½ TABLESPOONS BAKING SODA, MEASURING CUP, ½ CUP VINEGAR, ¼ CUP WARM WATER, PLASTIC ZIPPER BAG

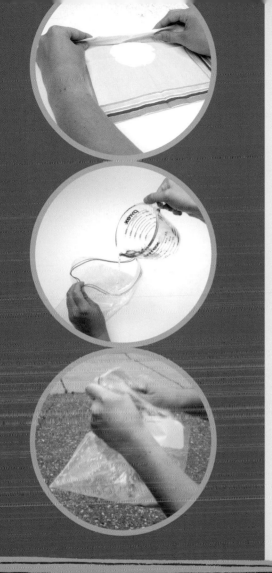

HOW TO DO IT

1 Unfold the napkin. Put the baking soda on the napkin. Roll the napkin up tightly.

2 Pour the vinegar and water into the plastic bag. Close the zipper halfway.

3 Go outside. Put the napkin in the bag. Seal it quickly.

4 Shake the bag. Set it on the ground. Move a few feet away. Watch as your bicarbonate bomb goes boom!

WHAT'S HAPPENING?

In this experiment, baking soda is a **base**. Vinegar is an **acid**. The base and the acid react together. Your kidneys keep the acids and bases in your body balanced.

WATER

W ater is important for staying healthy! You need to drink water every day.

Your kidneys help your body keep the right amount of water. Your kidneys tell your brain when you need water. You feel thirsty.

If you have too much water, your kidneys **filter** it out.

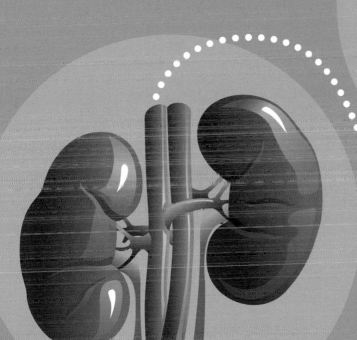

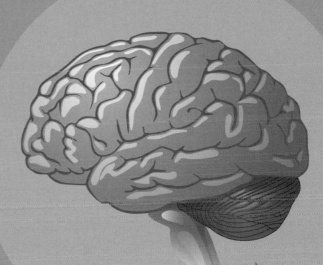

I'M THIRSTY!

URINE

Your kidneys **filter** your blood. The good stuff stays behind. The waste goes out. The waste is called urine (YOOR-uhn). It is also called pee.

RESTROOM

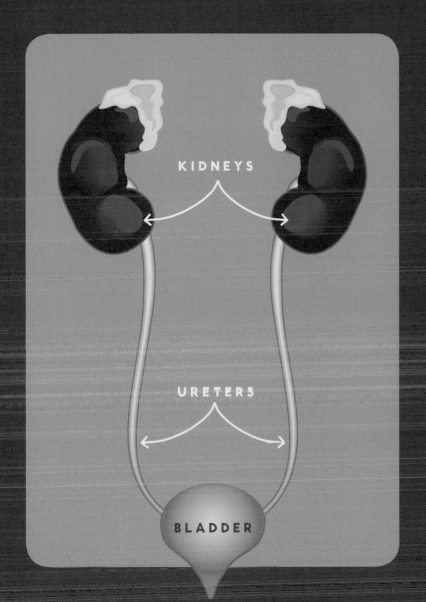

KIDNEYS

URETERS

BLADDER

The urine goes through tubes called ureters (*yoor-EE-turz*). The tubes connect to the **bladder**.

Your bladder tells your brain when it is full. Your brain tells you to go to the bathroom! The bladder **squeezes**. The urine flows out through another tube. It is called the urethra (*yoo-REE-thruh*).

WHY IS URINE YELLOW?

U rine is mostly water. But it has salts and waste too. The yellow color comes from urochrome (*YOOR-uh-krohm*). It is part of the waste from your blood.

WHAT IS URINE MADE OF?

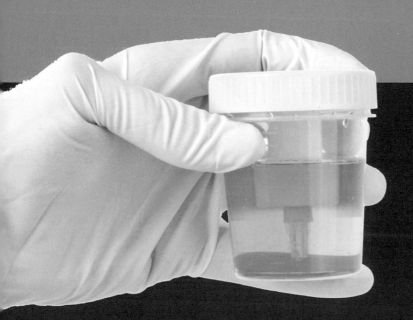

5% SALTS AND WASTE

95% WATER

The smell of urine comes from ammonia (*uh-MOHN-yuh*). Ammonia is also waste from your blood.

Sometimes what we eat changes the color of our urine. Beets can turn it pink! **Asparagus** can turn it green!

MODEL MAKER

MODEL YOUR KIDNEYS!

WHAT YOU NEED: JAR WITH METAL LID, NAIL, HAMMER, 24 INCHES (61 CM) OF PLASTIC TUBING, RULER, SCISSORS, CLAY, COTTON BALLS, MEASURING CUP, MEASURING SPOONS, GLITTER, FUNNEL, DUCT TAPE, DRINKING GLASS

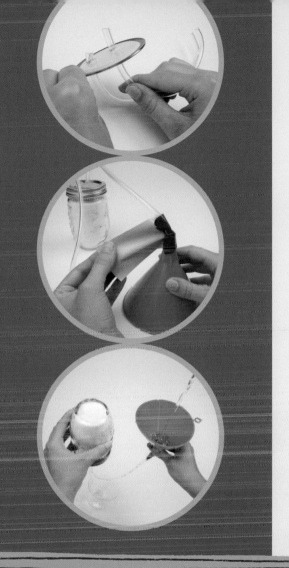

HOW TO DO IT

1. Take the lid off the jar. Use the hammer and nail to make two holes in the lid. Cut the tubing in half. Push one end of each tube through a hole.

2. Fill the holes around the tubes with clay. Fill the jar with cotton balls. Put the lid on the jar.

3. Fill the measuring cup with water. Add 1 teaspoon of glitter.

4. Tape the tip of the funnel to one of the tubes.

5. Hold the jar upside down. Hold the funnel higher than the jar. Put the other tube in a glass. Have a friend pour the water into the funnel.

WHAT'S HAPPENING?

The water is your blood. The jar is your kidney. The jar **filters** the water. It catches the stuff your body needs. That is the glitter. The stuff your body doesn't need goes through the kidneys. It comes out as urine.

VITAMIN D

Vitamin D makes your bones strong. Vitamin D comes from the sun and some foods. It travels through your blood. Your kidneys change vitamin D into the form your bones can use!

FOODS THAT HAVE VITAMIN D

MUSHROOMS

TOFU

CAVIAR

MILK

SALMON

BUTTER

EGGS

TUNA

SWISS CHEESE

Vitamin D is important. Make sure you get enough! But you should still wear sunscreen if you are in the sun more than 30 minutes. It protects your skin from sunburn.

EPO

TO THE RESCUE

Your blood needs red blood cells. Your bones make red blood cells. A special **messenger** tells your bones to make red blood cells. It is erythropoietin. It's called EPO for short. Guess what makes EPO? Your kidneys!

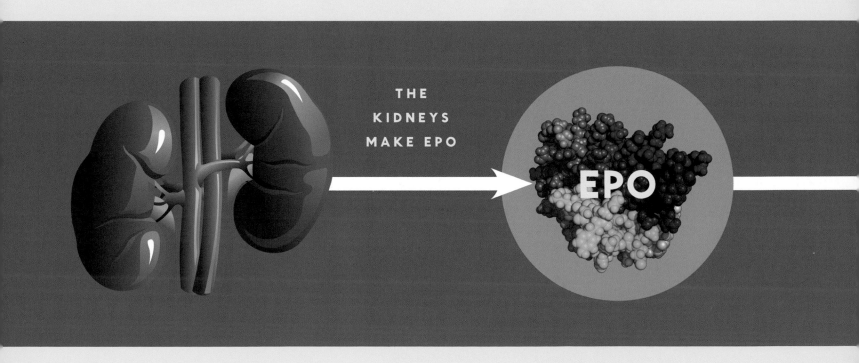

THE KIDNEYS MAKE EPO

EPO

Try to say it! It's not easy!

E-RYTH-RO-POI-E-TIN
(i-RITH-roh-POI-uh-ten)

EPO GOES INTO BONES

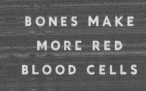

BONES MAKE MORE RED BLOOD CELLS

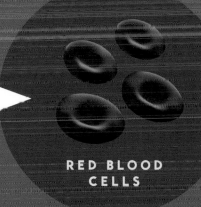

RED BLOOD CELLS

KIDNEY HEALTH

Your kidneys need water to work well. So drink liquids every day. Water, milk, and juice are great choices.

Bring a water bottle when you play outside or go for a hike.

Let It Flow!

Don't hold your pee in! When you have to go, go as soon as you can! This keeps your kidneys healthy.

ACID - a type of chemical that reacts when mixed with a base.

ASPARAGUS - a green plant that grows spear-shaped stalks that can be cooked and eaten.

BASE - a type of chemical that reacts when mixed with an acid.

BLADDER - the organ in the body that stores urine.

BLOOD VESSEL - one of the tubes that carry blood throughout the body.

FILTER - 1. something that separates parts of a liquid. 2. to clean with a filter.

GALLON - a unit for measuring liquids. Milk and gasoline are often sold by the gallon.

MESSENGER - someone or something that carries a message from one place to another.

SQUEEZE - to press or grip something tightly.

GLOSSARY